Our Earth
How Kids are Saving the Planet

written and illustrated by Janet Wilson

Second Story Press

Dedicated to my grandson, Leon,
my reminder of why we need to care for our Earth,
and to young environmental activists.
You are the generation we have been waiting for.

If many little people,
in many little places,
do many little things,
they can change
the face of the Earth.

(African Proverb)

The Rainbow Warriors

There will be a time when the animals and
the giant trees will begin to disappear.
People will fight with each other and not love each other.
The beautiful rainbow in the sky will fade away.
Then children will come,
children who will love the animals, and who will bring
back the animals.
They will love trees,
and they will bring back the giant trees.
These children will love other people
and they will help people to
live in peace with each other.
These children will love the rainbow,
and they will bring back the beautiful
rainbow in the sky.
They will be called
the Rainbow Warriors.

Do you love animals?
Do you love trees?
Do you love people?
Do you love the rainbow?
Well, if you do, maybe you
are a Rainbow Warrior.

Every living thing shares one home – our Earth.

Creatures that dive, creep, slither, or soar all breathe the same air. Branches, petals, and sprouts reach toward the same sun. Whether we dance on two legs, or gallop on four, all of Earth's children need water to live.

Today, Earth is showing signs of strain from the rapid increase in the number of us who live on it and from how we use our planet's precious gifts. Many Aboriginal cultures around the world tell ancient stories, such as the Rainbow Warriors, that predict these alarming changes to Earth. They warn that we need to change our ways. Since the time that he was chosen as Keeper of the Sacred Peace Pipe when he was twelve, Chief Arvol Looking Horse of the Lakota Sioux Nation has been spreading this message around the world: "Our vision is for peoples of all continents to come together as one; to heal and restore peace, harmony, and balance to Earth, our Mother."

Why do these stories tell of children coming from each corner of the globe to save Earth? I believe it's because young people have many important qualities that are essential to care for Earth. They adapt more easily to change and are flexible in mind and heart. Youth have time, energy, and enthusiasm. Young people also have strength in numbers – nearly half of Earth's population is young. This generation is more educated and interconnected globally than any other has ever been. This is a generation that is capable of developing informed opinions and understanding of the issues concerning their future.

Perhaps the most important power young people share is their love of nature. Although today's youth spend more time indoors than the young people of previous generations, there is a growing movement to get out and reconnect with our precious Earth. Young people with visions of a smarter and healthier world are finding ways to be part of the solution.

They are our Rainbow Warriors.

—Janet Wilson

"I'm only a child and I don't have all the solutions but neither do you!"

Severn is called "the girl who silenced the world for five minutes."

When she was nine, Severn spent the summer in a remote Kayapo Indian village in the Amazon rainforest. Kayapo friends showed her where turtles hid their eggs in the sand and how to catch electric eels. They took long walks together, ate just-picked papaya for lunch, and splashed in the river where little piranhas swam. From the plane window on her way home, Severn was devastated to see large fires destroying the rainforest. Her outrage motivated her to raise money with some friends so that they could attend an important environmental conference in Rio de Janeiro, Brazil. There she was able to deliver a speech to world leaders. She spoke passionately, telling them, "You don't know how to fix the holes in our ozone layer. You don't know how to bring salmon back up a dead stream. You don't know how to bring back an animal now extinct, and you can't bring back forests that once grew where there is now desert. If you don't know how to fix it, please stop breaking it!" Some people in the audience cried; others stood and applauded. Many thought it was the best speech at the conference.

Listen to Severn's speech on www.youtube.com

Severn says:

Young people have a special power – pester power. Your parents love you, so tell them your fears and concerns. Recruit them to be eco-warriors.

"I speak for all generations to come... on behalf of starving children around the world and for the countless animals dying. I am afraid to go out in the sun because of the holes in the ozone, or to breathe the air because I don't know what chemicals are in it, and for animals and plants going extinct every day. Did you have to worry about these things when you were my age? I'm only a child yet I know if all the money spent on war was spent on ending poverty and finding environmental answers, what a wonderful place this Earth would be! You teach us to behave in the world, not to fight with others, to work things out, to respect others, to clean up our mess, not to hurt other creatures, to share, and not be greedy. Then why do you go out and do the things you tell us not to do? You grownups say you love us. I challenge you; please make your actions reflect your words."
Earth Summit, Brazil, 1992.

William Kamkwamba, 14, Malawi

"My dream is to be an engineer so I can make the world a better place starting with my village."

William, atop his windmill in Masitala village, Malawi

When his family's small farm didn't earn enough money to pay his tuition fees, William had to leave school. Luckily, he was still allowed to use the library. William borrowed a book called *Using Energy* and read that a windmill generated electricity, something his village really needed. An electric water pump would irrigate the crops so villagers would not starve. Lights would be better than the smoky paraffin candles that made his sisters cough. William longed to hear music and news on a radio. He decided a windmill was the answer.

William collected everything he could find – a broken bicycle, a fan and headlights from an old tractor, pipes, wires, rusty nails, a shock absorber, scrap timber, even rubber flip-flops. He studied the photo of a windmill on the cover of the book and started to work.

The villagers came to watch. "He must be going crazy!" they said. Six months later, they gathered around the 16-foot (5-meter) tall windmill as William flicked a switch. For the first time, electric light shone in the village of Masitala

Read more about William at
www.williamkamkwamba.typepad.com

William says:

We should help provide everyday people with the means to improve their own lives, to have food, clean water, medicine, and education for children so they will grow up with a good foundation.

William's first windmill generated enough electricity to power four lights, two radios, and a mobile phone charger. William built three more windmills, one to power a water pump. As news of the windmills grew, William was invited to speak at conferences. He returned to school, and eventually the proceeds from his book, *The Boy Who Harnessed the Wind*, built an environmentally sustainable school in his village. Now other young people are learning how to make windmills and fix water pumps for the village.

Kassabian, Nigeria

Energy comes in many forms – heat, light, sound, and motion are just a few. Energy can be converted to produce wind power from turbines, combustion of oil and gasoline, and electricity for many purposes.

"Look! The magic is all around you – in nature, plants, flowers, and in all the animals that share the planet with us."

Young Kruti, performing her magic

Kruti Parekh is a world famous young magician with a message: Saving the planet is not an illusion. "It is my life's mission to use my magic to heal Earth of its tragic wounds caused by environmental degradation," she says. Kruti started practicing magic when she was five. By the time she was thirteen, she had become India's youngest professional magician. Kruti believes kids need a good environmental education, but because lectures can sometimes be boring, she uses fantastic tricks to promote awareness. In one, Kruti turns herself into a recycling machine. She swallows huge wads of waste paper and then pulls from her mouth long strands of colored paper. "You see, if we discard paper in the right way, we can use it again!"

Kruti can make a helicopter and elephants vanish to encourage people to think that anything is possible. She convinced a huge festival in India that the thousands of flowers used for decoration should be turned into compost for fertilizer instead of being thrown into the sea. Kruti tours the world with her environmental magic shows and has won many awards.

Find out more about Kruti at www.magiciankruti.com

Kruti says:

We need to reduce, reuse, and recycle our waste, but also rethink what we really need and refuse what we don't. Cleaning up the environment is not one person's job. We all need to join hands to make a difference.

Kruti supports an eco-friendly school in Mumbai to help 1,000 slum children have a brighter future. She aso founded Eco-Kids' Club so that youth in more than 100 schools can participate in conservation and recycling.

Plastic waste is a poison in the heart of Earth's ecosystem. Almost everything we buy is packaged in petroleum-based plastic, which is made to last forever and yet designed to be disposable. Millions of tons of plastic trash ends up in landfill or is dumped in oceans where it washes up on beaches or accumulates in gyres - massive, slow rotating whirlpools - creating floating islands of plastic. The Pacific garbage patch is larger than Texas.

"The clear and simple messages of children are more powerful than that of any adult."

Felix shows off saplings at the launch of Plant for the Planet

Felix Finkbeiner stood in front of his grade four class to explain global warming and its effects on the future of all children. "Carbon emissions are causing the temperature of the atmosphere to rise. Trees produce oxygen and reduce carbon emissions that lead to climate change. That's why I support the Billion Tree Campaign by planting trees in Germany." Felix showed a photo of the African woman who inspired this campaign sponsored by the United Nations Environmental Program. "If Wangari Maathai can plant thirty million trees, the children of Germany can plant one." The class cheered. His teacher suggested that they plant the tree at the entrance to the school. Felix corrected her. "I meant one million trees!" To raise support and motivate others to help, Felix started an organization called Plant for the Planet. He began speaking through the media and within two years, the children of Germany had reached their goal. Felix believes that talking about it is not enough to stop the glaciers from melting. The new campaign, Stop Talking, Start Planting, aims to have children plant one million trees in every country in the world.

Learn more at www.plant-for-the-planet.org

Felix says:

The children of the world demand climate justice – a fair distribution of power and resources. We should take responsibility for the pollution we cause. The more we use, the more we should replace. Each tree we plant is a symbol for climate justice. The more trees we plant, the more adults will pay attention to us!

"I would like young people to know that despite the challenges they face, there is hope. I have a lot of hope in youth. Their minds do not have to be held back by old thinking about the environment. Protecting the environment is not just a pleasure, but also a duty." —Wangari Maathai, winner of the Nobel Peace Prize for the Green Belt Movement.

Young Climate Ambassadors demonstrate in front of the government headquarters in Berlin, Germany.

The United Nations Billion Tree Campaign: By the end of 2009, more than 7.4 billion trees had been planted by participants in 170 countries.

Adeline Tiffanie Suwana, 12, Indonesia

"Nature and all its elements are precious treasures for young people."

Adeline and friends saving sea turtles, Indonesia

On December 26, 2004, horrified people around the world watched the devastating effects of a tsunami in Southeast Asia. Adeline Tiffanie Suwana became deeply concerned about the increase of flooding, hurricanes, and pollution affecting Indonesia, and all the ocean islands of the world. This motivated her to learn more about marine ecosystems and other important environmental issues. She learned that climate change contributes to natural disasters that will affect approximately 175 million children every year over the next decade. To show young people practical ways to help their Earth, Adeline founded *Sahabat Alam*, (Friends of Nature). "It is important to reinforce at an early stage a sense of love and caring towards the environment, because the future of the world will be in our hands," Adeline explains. More than 1,700 members are planting coral in damaged reefs and creating mangroves to help prevent damage from hurricanes and tsunamis. They also help with fish breeding, turtle protection, and volunteer for beach cleanups. Adeline presents her ideas to schools, cooperates with government agencies, has recorded a song about conservation, and is producing a TV program.

Check out www.sahabat-alam.com

Adeline says:

Earth is getting older and tired of having all of us. If we love our Earth, Earth will love us, but if we don't take care of our Earth, we will destroy it. Celebrate Earth Day on April 22, and every day. Help clean up the world. It's more fun if you volunteer with friends.

Nathania Candra, 11, Indonesia

"We have always had flooding here in Bangladesh, but in recent years it has become much worse. It seems like there's something wrong with nature. I'm scared that my whole village will disappear. I'm also scared of dying."
—Rebeka Aktar, 14, Bangladesh

Oceans cover 70% of the planet. Half of the world's population live near the coast. They will suffer the effects of rising sea levels due to melting glaciers. Eleven percent of the world's coral reefs already have been destroyed and 16% are badly damaged. Many species of marine animals are facing extinction due to pollution and over-fishing.

Ryan Hreljac, 7, Canada

"You can make a difference in the world, but only if you really try hard and really want to. Just pick a dream and then go for it."

Ryan, 15, checks one of his wells in Uganda

When Ryan Hreljac was in grade one, his teacher told the class that children in poor countries, such as in Africa, often had to walk miles every day to get water from the nearest well. Ryan counted the number of steps it took him to reach the nearest tap – only ten. He filled a glass with clear, clean water, remembering that many children get sick and die from drinking dirty water. It did not seem fair to Ryan that children in rich countries had cleaner water than children in poor countries. He wanted to do something to help. What could one six-year-old do? Ryan decided that he could not help every poor child in Africa, but he could raise money to buy one well. Over the next few months, he earned $70 by doing chores. When he learned that amount would only buy a pump, Ryan's determination grew like ripples from a stone thrown into water. Ryan's dream inspired others to help raise the $2,000 needed to build his first well at a school in Uganda. Since then, Ryan's Well Foundation has raised millions of dollars and has created more than 500 water and sanitation projects in 16 countries.

To learn more, go to www.ryanswell.ca

Ryan says:

Be kind. Be compassionate. Care and share what you have with others. Get involved in your communities and in the world.

Almost 80% of diseases in developing countries are associated with unsafe water. Each year 1.5 million children under five die from water-borne diseases. The demand for clean water is increasing as the world's population grows by about 80 million annually. For humans and ecosystems to thrive, water must be clean, and be available to all. The world currently spends $15 billion a year on water supply and sanitation. Compare that to an estimated $100 billion spent on water bottled in plastic. One third of that money could secure a source of clean drinking water for another 500 million people and prevent over 36 billion bottles a year going to landfill.

Emelyanova Inna Wladimrovna, Russia, won a UN environmental art competition for this work.

Sam Levin, 15, USA

"We will be the generation that reunites mankind with the Earth."

Sam, 15, in the Project Sprout garden

Sam Levin was happiest when he was getting his hands dirty – digging potatoes in the black soil at his grandpa's farm, playing soccer with piglets, catching toads in swamps, and picking fiddleheads in the woods. When he was thirteen, Sam learned that his favorite small farms and wild places were quickly disappearing. This gave him the idea for Project Sprout – a student-run, organic vegetable garden aimed at building connections with nature and food. Sam took his idea to his guidance counselor. Together with students Sarah Steadman and Natalie Akers, they worked out a plan. One year later, Project Sprout's garden supplied the school's cafeteria with fresh fruits and vegetables, donated over 1,000 pounds (450 kg) of produce for needy families, and served as a living laboratory for students. The next year the garden tripled in size and added an orchard. Sam believes the project succeeded because of the group's motivation, energy, and sense of hope. "Youth is the most powerful force in our country right now. Sarah, Natalie and I are not special. Slowly we proved to ourselves and others that we were organized, dedicated, and had thought through the challenges we would face."

Find out more at www.edibleschoolyard.org

Sam says:

Pay more attention to where your food comes from and how it's grown. Buy fair trade products that ensure fair wages for workers in poorer areas, as well as healthy social and environmental practices during the production of goods. Try to eat 'real' food in season that is grown locally, and isn't grown with pesticides. If you eat meat, eat less of it.

Students gardening at Monument Mountain High School, Great Barrington, Massachusetts, USA

Raising animals for food generates more greenhouse gases than all the cars and trucks in the world combined. The meat industry is one of the most significant contributors to today's most serious environmental problems including deforestation. Studies show that producing meat requires more than eight times as much fossil-fuel energy as producing plant protein. Vegetarians choose not to eat meat and believe they get all necessary nutrients from plants alone.

Janine Licare, 13, Costa Rica

"We should do anything we can to save the rainforests...
they're the storehouses of treasures on Earth."

Janine, 13, with a rehabilitated dwarf raccoon

Janine Licare and her friend Aislin Livingstone were only nine when they decided to earn some spending money by selling painted rocks to tourists by the side of the road. But as they watched rainforest trees being cut down and tiny Titi monkeys struggling to cross the busy road, they decided to spend the money on rope to build overhead monkey bridges. But they wanted to do even more to save their vanishing rainforest and endangered animals and plants. To get others to help, Janine and Aislin started Kids Saving the Rainforest. They opened a store to sell their own arts and crafts and the work of local artists. All the profits go to buying monkey bridges, preserving rainforest land, planting trees, rehabilitating injured sloths, kinkajous and other baby animals. KSR is raising money to build an Education Center in the Manuel Antonio rainforest to educate people about rainforests and the connection between humans and nature. Trees stabilize the world's climate, purify the air we breathe, provide homes for most of the plants and animals, and are a vital source of medicine, food, and building materials. Trees protect against flood, drought and erosion; cutting them leads to desertification.

To learn more go to www.kidssavingtherainforest.org

Janine says:

Learn, learn, learn! Learn what products come from the rainforest and decide if you really need to buy them. Support eco-tourism and rainforest conservation. We have to be the generation that makes a difference!

Janeth Paucar, Challabaneba, Peru

"Can't we just buy some rainforest?" **Roland Tiensuu**, 12, Sweden. The first child-led movement to save a rainforest began in 1988 when students at Fagervik School learned that rainforests were destroyed for the logging and cattle industries at a rate of 100 acres a minute. Earth has already lost at least 80% of its original forests. On average, logging and cattle ranching will drive 137 life species into extinction every day. The students raised $25,000 to establish the International Children's Rainforest of Costa Rica. Since then young activists from around the world have raised millions of dollars to preserve rainforests.

Fang Minghe, 17, China

"People have different eye colors...I hope one day, people will have green eyes to help them see a much greener world."

Minghe meets his hero, animal behavior pioneer Jane Goodall

Fang Minghe puts on his Green Eyes China cap, grabs the video camera, and rushes out the door to meet his friends at an outdoor market. They maneuver through the crowds, plastic bins, and crates full of animals. Minghe wants to free the animals, but today the Green Eyes group is looking for endangered breeds of frogs, snakes, owls, and eagles. When they spot illegal wildlife being sold for a cooking pot, pet food, or traditional Chinese medicine, Minghe secretly films the evidence. If the sellers see him, they often get angry, deny the animals belong to them, or run away. But with the videos, Minghe has the proof the police need for their investigation.

Minghe's deep love and compassion for all life began when he was young and living in the countryside. His closest friends were animals, so when he first saw photos of animals tortured and slain by poachers, he recruited twelve human friends to form the Green Eyes Club to protect animals and the environment. Now, more than 5,000 members across China report polluters, help with cleanups, run animal sanctuaries and rescue centers, and lecture in schools.

For more information go to www.greeneyeschina.org

Minghe says:

Commit yourself to action, for the fate of the Earth lies not in government hands, but in our hands. The greatest danger to Earth is for people to stand by and not do anything.

Baby chimpanzee eating greens, Gombe forest, Tanzania

Minghe was inspired by Jane Goodall, the animal behavior pioneer who spent her life studying chimpanzees in Africa. Her Roots and Shoots foundation is dedicated to the well being of all living things. She explains: "Roots creep underground and make a firm foundation. Shoots seem very weak, but to reach the light, they can break open brick walls. Imagine that the brick walls are all the problems we have inflicted on our planet. Hundreds of thousands of roots and shoots, hundreds of thousands of young people around the world, can break through these walls. We CAN change the world."

Aika Tsubota, 12, Japan

"We will be the ones to protect the Earth
and solve the problems of wars, hunger, and disasters."

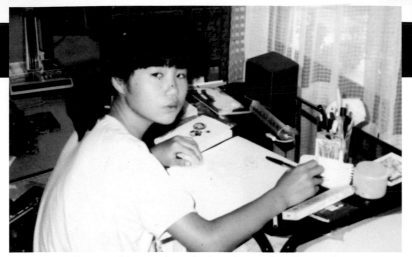

Aika, working at her desk at home in Hirata-city

Aika Tsubota had always felt one with the universe one with Earth, and all life. She had a gift for expressing her love of nature in words and art. She decided to make a comic book about the environment for a grade six assignment. Deeply concerned about the problems facing Earth, Aika wanted to explain these issues so that children could understand. Secretly she dreamed of publishing her comic. For two months Aika researched, wrote, and drew the storyboards, sometimes late into the night. On December 25, 1991, Aika handed in *Secrets of the Earth*. Hours later, she developed a severe headache and collapsed. Aika died two days later. At her funeral, her parents gave copies of the comic to Aika's classmates. More people wanted to read it and eventually Aika's dream came true – *Secrets of the Earth* was published.

When she was ten, Aika wrote, "I would like to become an Earth that is powerful, gentle to cradle, and fosters all of the lives on it." Perhaps Aika is watching over the future of Earth.

To read *Secrets of the Earth* in English, go to: www.scribd.com/doc/17543062/Secrets-of-the-Earth

Aika said:

The most important thing is for people to stop thinking they can't do anything just because they are only one individual. If everybody thought that way, Earth really would be doomed! If everybody pitches in, I know we can turn this planet into a beautiful place.

Yesterday is what grownups did.
Tomorrow is what kids will do.
Throwing cans away is the past.
Picking them up is the future.
Throwing cans away is light.
Picking them up is heavy.
—Aika Tsubota

Aika Tsubota, 12, Japan

In *Secrets of the Earth*, Planet Earth teaches a boy and girl about its history, natural wonders, resources, and the problems of climate change, pollution, endangered species, and global warming. By the end the characters are "raring to go to protect the Earth!"

Kids Take Action!

Cool Youth

"Adults say, 'It's great to have kids involved. You are the future.' We're more than just the future. We're the present. We can make a difference now. We don't have to wait until we're grown up. Let's work together now to change the world."
Alec Loorz, USA, was 12 when he founded Kids Versus Global Warming to teach the science of global warming and empower youth to take action. To show that global warming is causing the polar ice to melt, the kids installed poles along the Californian coast and marked lines on them to show people how much the ocean will rise if nothing is done to curb the current rate of global warming.

Alec Loorz, 14, with his first sea level awareness pole, Ventura Beach boardwalk, California

"When I was fifteen, I saw the white spirit bear in its dark forest green backdrop – it was awe-inspiring, reminding me why it is so important to save this wilderness."

Simon Jackson, Canada, founded the Spirit Bear Youth Coalition to raise awareness of the rare, endangered white bear. His campaign started with some students writing letters and became the world's largest youth-run environmental organization with a network in 74 countries. Some of Hollywood's top animators are making a full-length movie, *The Spirit Bear*, to raise money.
www.spiritbearyouth.org

"If the air looks bad and smells bad, it probably is bad - even a six-year-old can understand that."
Illai Kenney, 12, USA, co-founded Georgia Kids Against Pollution to protest 13 dirty coal-fired plants that were dumping asthma-causing air pollutants into the poor neighborhoods of Atlanta. Illai was the youngest delegate invited to the United Nations where she spoke about the connection between poverty and the environment.

Twelve-year-old **Haruka Maruno** loved her dog Patrick, but picking up his poop with a plastic bag was gross – and bad for the environment. The poop decomposed naturally but the plastic did not. Japan has millions of dogs; Haruka was concerned about all that plastic ending up in landfill. She invented a hands-off "Haruka's Paperscoop" from a biodegradable milk carton.

"Having cancer was a terrible experience, but this struggle taught me to accept my responsibilities as a member of the community. We can make a difference and do something to help children." After learning that his cancer may have been caused by exposure to the huge amounts of pesticides used to keep area golf courses green, Canadian **Jean-Dominic Lévesque-René**, 10, convinced his local government to force golf courses to reduce their use of pesticides. He extended his protest throughout North America, winning support for both his cause and his fight over cancer.

Pester Power!

When young people learned that millions of dolphins were dying in tuna nets, they began talking to their parents. **Ashley Biden**, 8, convinced her dad, Joe Biden, who was then a US senator and became Vice President, to introduce a law requiring canned tuna labels to state if dolphins had died in the catch. One tuna company changed their nets after the chairman's own children urged him to stop the killing of dolphins. If you want to be a peaceful website warrior to save dolphins go to www.idw.org

"All children want a rainforest to be there when we grow up. Please act – act now!" When **Omar Castillo Gallegos** was 8, he learned about the destruction of the last rainforest in the Mexican state of Chiapas. He walked for 39 days and 800 miles (1,287 km) from his home in Mexico City to speak to the governor. Omar was told to return home to talk to the president. He pitched a tent outside the palace, and shouted, "I want to see the president so he will save the rainforest!" Other people joined Omar, attracting attention from the media, and, finally, the president met with Omar and promised to save the rainforest. Although that promise was broken, Omar's actions successfully raised awareness of the rainforest destruction.

Omar Castillo with Protect The Forest sign outside the presidential palace, Mexico City.

Kids Create!

"I was inspired to create because we all share Earth's finite resources and revel in its beauty. We can't just stand by while our brothers and sisters die from freak storms or rising sea levels. We can't leave a damaged and dying world to our children who will feel the major effects of climate change when we are all gone. We only have one Earth."
—**Slater Jewell-Kemker**, 15, Canada/USA is an award-winning short filmmaker. Her work includes *An Inconvenient Youth* and *Don't Give It All Away*.

Paula Chacin, Venezuela, has created a photo gallery of polluted sites from around her city to raise awareness of the environmental damage taking place.

A major cause of illness is polluted water where most children swim

Rap for the Planet

"Turn off your lights, save electricity/Change our planet into something pretty/Going to work by yourself in an SUV?/You should go with H-Y-B-R-I-D/If you can't afford that, go with public transit/Take your bike, run, walk, jog, It'll make you fit".
—**Darrick Lee** (D-Pain) and **Michael Darnel** (Phat Mike), 16, Canada, performed "Hurting our Planet" at the Tunza Conference on the Environment in South Korea, 2009, for more than 200 young people from 100 countries.

Art Takes A Bus Ride

Kevin Huo, 10, USA was the grand prize winner of a California public transit art competition. His work was wrapped around a bus to inspire people to take public transit and help the planet. "One bus can take 45 cars off the road," he says.

Eleanor Sutcliffe was 11 years old when she asked other kids to help her clean the trash that was spoiling their seaside beaches in Wales. From the rubbish, they created beauty, making public sculptures. She created the Save Our Seas, Wales, agency. Once a week, they clean beaches and make a note of every single bit of garbage to send to the marine conservation society for its environmental data bank. Eleanor says, "I used to be teased at school, but after I started SOS I have made so many new friends".

Eleanor Sutcliffe, UK, Young Marine Conservationist
with beach trash sculptures

It's haunting me/A crowd of he's and she's
I'm not a hero/I'm not even a big show
Every time I look/Cameras are flashing me in the eye.
It would surprise them if they knew/I was only a little girl
who is scared the world will die
—**Bambou Chieppas**, 11, Indonesia, read her poem at the UN International Climate Change Conference, where 180 countries gathered in Bali, Indonesia, 2007. UNICEF called it the launch of the global youth environment movement.

"Habits made today will help life tomorrow" is the motto of Australian **Parrys Raines**, Youth Ambassador for WWF (World Wide Fund for Nature). As Climate Girl, 14-year-old Parrys writes blogs to inform young people about the positive things young people can do to help locally, to create hope rather than distress.
www.climategirl.com.au

Ludmila Balovneva, 9, Russia, won the UNEP 2009 Global Painting Competition on the Environment over more than two million entries. "Where I live, everything is polluted. There is broken glass and rubbish everywhere. And the trees get cut down. I wanted to depict two ways of developing the world. The clean way and the dirty way. It's about the future."

How You Can Help

Take the Tunza Pledge!

Youth attending the Tunza Conference in Korea, 2009.

As young, caring citizens of this planet, we commit ourselves to restoring and preserving our world, and to rebuilding our dreams of tomorrow – pure waters, vast wild lands, clean air, and cities free from poverty.

Tunza is an African word meaning to treat with care or affection. The TUNZA Youth Strategy was created by the United Nations Environmental Program (UNEP) to foster a generation of green conscious citizens. For more information go to www.tunza.org

Start or Join a Club

"Although climate change is a big problem and a big challenge, it is also an opportunity for our generation to change the world through our actions. We need to think big and come up with large system-changing ideas and actions."
—**Annie Collins**, 12, Canada, started the Sustainability Club at her school in Nakusp, BC. They serve and sell fair trade products, give educational presentations, have a school garden, and install bike racks to encourage students to cycle to school.

Practice Pester Power

Write letters or speak to your leaders. **Yugratna Srivastava**, 13, India, spoke to more than 100 world leaders, including US President Barack Obama and UN Secretary General Ban Ki-Moon, at a 2009 conference on climate change. Here's what she said: *"Please listen to our voices. The future needs strong vision and leadership! Whatever has happened in the past is over. Let's act in the present to secure our future. Three billion young people need the leaders to act now! We received a clean and healthy planet from our ancestors and we are gifting a damaged one to our successors. What sort of justice is this? Gandhi said 'Earth has enough to satisfy everyone's need but no one's greed.' A bird can fly, a fish can swim, a leopard can run, but humans have a mind capable to think, change and reform. So let us all use these abilities to save our Mother Earth!"*

Save the Planet

Get Unplugged!

Do you have Nature Deficit Disorder? Young people only spend half the time outdoors that young people did 20 years ago. North American youth spend an average of six hours per day on electronic media. This increases the likelihood of attention-deficit disorder, obesity, stress, impaired social skills, asthma, and poorer school performance.

Cory Wilson

Raise Awareness

When **Cameron Oliver**, 12, United Arab Emirates, learned that camels were dying from eating plastic litter, he began raising awareness in the media, giving presentations, and creating T-shirts, bumper stickers, and a website. "I want my children to see live camels and not read about them in books," Cameron says. www.cameronscamelcampaign.com

Give your school an e-report card

Schools leave large ecological footprints. The Green Schools Program encourages students to conduct an inspection or survey of their school and rate and reduce its footprint to create a healthier environment. To learn how to do a survey at your school, go to http://www.greenschools.net/form. php?modin=53

An average school lunch generates 67 pounds of waste per school year. Pack your food and liquids in reusable containers, add biodegradable fruits, use a cloth napkin and reusable cutlery, and don't buy over-packaged snacks.

Jin Ho Huh, 13, South Korea, makes bags to encourage people to use instead of plastic. A common estimate is that global consumption of plastic bags is from 500 billion to over a trillion plastic bags annually, almost 1 million plastic bags used per minute.

Alex Lin, 14, USA, installed the first ever e-waste receptacle in his town of Westerly, Rhode Island, and pushed for passage of laws banning the dumping of e-waste.

Acknowledgments

I appreciate all the amazing young activists who gave me permission to tell their stories. I extend heartfelt thanks to them and to their friends and family members who kindly provided information and photographs. Thanks, also, to the staff at UNEP and the other agencies who helped me, and to my many dear friends, I'm sorry that space does not permit me to mention everyone by name. My models were Cody Looking Horse, Dane Kirkpatrick, and Rowen Pilon. Thanks, also, to the Second Story team.

I am exceedingly grateful to the George Woodcock Writers' Trust and the Ontario Arts Council Writers' Reserve grant for the financial support that made it possible for me to create *Our Earth*.

Chris Wilson, my unsung hero and partner in work and life, provided invaluable help as master sleuth, computer wizard, chief cook, editor, researcher, and much more.

Credits:

The Rainbow Warriors is adapted from a version of traditional Aboriginal oral history attributed to a telling by Lelanie Stone.

Severn: Photo left: Arlen Redekop/*The Province*. Photo right: video photo courtesy of The Environmental Children's Organization

William: Photo ©Tom O'Reilly. Art courtesy of Paint for the Planet, an exhibit of youth art from UNEP International Children's Painting Competition, UNite to Combat Climate Change. Depicting children's fears and hopes for the planet, the paintings are a powerful plea for leadership on climate change.

Kruti: Photo left courtesy of Kruti Parekh. Photo right ©Anna Cummins.

Felix: Photos courtesy of Michael Setzpfandt, Plant For The Planet

The Green Belt Movement was a grassroots tree-planting program to address the challenges of deforestation, soil erosion and lack of water.

Adeline: Photo courtesy of Sahabat Alam. Art courtesy of International Children's Art Foundation www.icaf.org

Ryan: Photo courtesy of Ryan's Well Foundation. Art: winner, Paint for the Planet, courtesy of UNEP.

Water statistics from: United Nations Report 2006 & United Nations World Water Development Report 3, presented ahead of the Fifth World Water Forum in Istanbul (Turkey) from 16 to 22 March.

Sam: All photos courtesy of Sam Levin, Project Sprout.

Janine: Photo courtesy of Jennifer Rice. Art: 1st-3rd grade group winner of the youth drawing and painting contest "Protecting and valuing our natural and cultural environment" by the Amazon Conservation Association, by permission. www.amazonconservation.org

Minghe: Photo left courtesy of Xiu Min Li and Green Eyes China. Photo right by permission of Rob Sassor, JGI.

Aika: photo courtesy of Youko Tsubota. Art from *Secrets of the Earth*.

Kids Take Action: Photo left courtesy of Virginia Loorz. Photo center courtesy of D. Simon Jackson. Art: courtesy of International Dolphin Watch. Photo right courtesy of and published by Volcano Press (www.volcanopress.com) Pester Power logo courtesy Dr. Horace Dobbs.

Kids Create: Photo left courtesy of FEZU. Photo center courtesy of Kevin Huo and the Go Green Transit campaign of the San Mateo County Transit District. Art: courtesy of UNEP. Photo right courtesy of Eleanor Sutcliffe.

How You Can Help: Photo courtesy of UNEP. Logo courtesy of Cameron Oliver. Get Unplugged! illustration by Cory Wilson.

School lunch statistics from: research published by the Children and Nature Organization. Term "Nature Deficit Disorder" is from *Last Child in the Woods*, by Richard Louv.

Library and Archives Canada Cataloguing in Publication

Wilson, Janet, 1952-
Our earth : how kids are saving the planet / written and
illustrated by Janet Wilson.

ISBN 978-1-897187-84-5

1. Child environmentalists—Biography—Juvenile literature.
I. Title.

GE55.W55 2010   j333.72092'2   C2010-902513-X

*Second Story Press gratefully acknowledges the support of
the Ontario Arts Council and the Canada Council for the Arts
for our publishing program. We acknowledge the financial
support of the Government of Canada through the Book
Publishing Industry Development Program.*

Printed and bound in China

 ONTARIO ARTS COUNCIL
CONSEIL DES ARTS DE L'ONTARIO

 Canada Council   Conseil des Arts
for the Arts   du Canada

Published by
Second Story Press
20 Maud Street, Suite 401
Toronto, Ontario, Canada
M5V 2M5
www.secondstorypress.ca

FSC
www.fsc.org
MIX
Paper from
responsible sources
FSC™ C019368